S0-AFQ-665

ROBERTO CLEMENTE

A Real-Life Reader Biography

Kimberly Garcia

Mitchell Lane Publishers, Inc.
P.O. Box 619
Bear, Delaware 19701
http://www.mitchelllane.com

Printing   1   2   3   4   5   6   7   8   9

Real-Life Reader Biographies

Paula Abdul	Christina Aguilera	Marc Anthony	Lance Armstrong
Drew Barrymore	Tony Blair	Brandy	Garth Brooks
Kobe Bryant	Sandra Bullock	Mariah Carey	Aaron Carter
Cesar Chavez	**Roberto Clemente**	Christopher Paul Curtis	Roald Dahl
Oscar De La Hoya	Trent Dimas	Celine Dion	Sheila E.
Gloria Estefan	Mary Joe Fernandez	Michael J. Fox	Andres Galarraga
Sarah Michelle Gellar	Jeff Gordon	Virginia Hamilton	Mia Hamm
Melissa Joan Hart	Salma Hayek	Jennifer Love Hewitt	Faith Hill
Hollywood Hogan	Katie Holmes	Enrique Iglesias	Allen Iverson
Janet Jackson	Derek Jeter	Steve Jobs	Alicia Keys
Michelle Kwan	Bruce Lee	Jennifer Lopez	Cheech Marin
Ricky Martin	Mark McGwire	Alyssa Milano	Mandy Moore
Chuck Norris	Tommy Nuñez	Rosie O'Donnell	Mary-Kate and Ashley Olsen
Rafael Palmeiro	Gary Paulsen	Colin Powell	Freddie Prinze, Jr.
Condoleezza Rice	Julia Roberts	Robert Rodriguez	J.K. Rowling
Keri Russell	Winona Ryder	Cristina Saralegui	Charles Schulz
Arnold Schwarzenegger	Selena	Maurice Sendak	Dr. Seuss
Shakira	Alicia Silverstone	Jessica Simpson	Sinbad
Jimmy Smits	Sammy Sosa	Britney Spears	Julia Stiles
Ben Stiller	Sheryl Swoopes	Shania Twain	Liv Tyler
Robin Williams	Vanessa Williams	Venus Williams	Tiger Woods

Library of Congress Cataloging-in-Publication Data
Garcia, Kimberly, 1966-
    Roberto Clemente / Kimberly Garcia.
        p. cm. — (A real-life reader biography)
    Includes index.
    Summary: A biography, emphasizing the philanthropic deeds as well as the athletic achievements, of the Hall of Fame baseball player from Puerto Rico who died in a plane crash in 1972.
    ISBN 1-58415-127-7 (lib)
        1. Clemente, Roberto, 1934-1972—Juvenile literature. 2. Baseball players—Puerto Rico—Biography—Juvenile literature. [1. Clemente, Roberto, 1934-1972. 2. Baseball players. 3. Puerto Ricans—Biography.] I. Title. II. Series.
GV865.C45 G25 2002
796.357'092—dc21
[B]
                                                                                                                        200202361

ABOUT THE AUTHOR: Kimberly Garcia is a bilingual journalist who found her first job at a newspaper on the U.S.--Mexico border because she spoke Spanish. Her paternal great grandparents migrated from Spain in the early 1900s to New York where her great grandfather edited an Anarchist newspaper. Garcia has a bachelor's degree in English and Spanish literature from the University of Wisconsin in Madison. After graduation, she worked six years as a daily newspaper journalist covering crime, local governments and Hispanic-related issues in Texas and Wisconsin. Garcia writes for *Hispanic, Vista,* and *Latina* magazines, among other publications. She currently lives in Austin, Texas.

PHOTO CREDITS: Cover: Globe Photos; p. 4 Archive Photos; p. 7, 8 Sporting News/Archive Photos; p. 12, 17, 19, 24 Bettmann/Corbis; p. 27 AP Photo; p. 29 AP Photo/Ray Stubblebine

128-1256

Table of Contents

Chapter 1
Getting Recognized

Roberto Clemente started the 1961 baseball season with a fire in his belly. During the previous season, he had helped the Pittsburgh Pirates win the World Series after a 33-year lapse. He thought his contributions made him a contender for Most Valuable Player of the National Baseball League. Instead, Clemente was gravely disappointed that sportswriters voted him the eighth best player. He was tired of not getting the recognition he thought he deserved. He was determined to win the batting title during the upcoming season to unmistakably show his talent. His resolve thrust him into the spotlight and

Clemente was tired of not getting the recognition he thought he deserved.

marked the beginning of a stunning five-year domination of major league baseball.

In 1961, Clemente burst out of the dugout swinging his bat more ferociously than ever, much to the dismay of players in his wake. On one occasion he hit a line drive that struck a reserve outfielder for the Pirates, Gino Cimoli, in the chest below the heart. The impact did not break any of Cimoli's bones, but Cimoli went to the hospital and was unable to play for several weeks. On another occasion, Clemente refused to let Don Drysdale intimidate him. Drysdale was a large pitcher for the Los Angeles Dodgers who was known for terrorizing batters with high, inside pitches. After one of Drysdale's fastballs forced Clemente to hit the deck, Clemente brushed himself off, got back in the batting box, and whacked another high, inside pitch over the outfield fence. As one sportswriter quipped, Clemente batted in 1961 as if the baseballs had "pictures of sportswriters painted on them."

Just as he had set out to do, Clemente won the batting title that year with a season average of .351, and that's not all. He also made his first appearance in an All-Star Game, and he took over Hank Aaron's place as the league's Gold Glove right fielder. He had played his most impressive defensive year, with a league and career high of 27 assists. After the 1961 season, no one could mistake Clemente's place among the finest players in the major leagues. He was a consistently powerful hitter and thrower from right field and was willing to sacrifice his body for the game.

Clemente was a consistently powerful hitter.

Clemente had finally arrived in the world of baseball, and the fun was just beginning. Fans back home in Puerto Rico were thrilled with his accomplishments and threw a triumphant welcome home party for him and Orlando Cepeda of the San Francisco Giants. Cepeda

Roberto celebrates his 3,000th hit

had scored the most home runs and batted in the most runs in the National League that same year. His and Clemente's feats made them the first Puerto Rican players to win any of the three main batting categories in either of the major leagues. Eighteen thousand cheering fans greeting them at the airport and lined the roads as they drove to a ceremony of 5,000 fans at the Sixto Escobar Stadium.

When Clemente returned to play baseball the following season, he continued to dominate the game, especially until 1966. He played between 144 and 155 games each year and batted an average of more than .310. He won three National League batting titles, six Gold Glove awards, and played in every All-Star Game. He also made his 1,000th base hit, against the Cincinnati Reds, in August 1961 and his 2,000th, against the Chicago Cubs, in September 1966. To put the icing on the cake, Clemente closed the best five years of his career by becoming the Most Valuable Player in 1966. He was proud to become the first Puerto Rican to win the title.

Even after Clemente's spectacular five years in baseball, he continued to shine. By the time his career ended in 1972, he had won four batting titles, a dozen Golden Glove awards, and two Most Valuable Player awards. He also helped the Pittsburgh Pirates win six division titles and two world championships. His finest moment was batting his 3,000th hit against the New York Mets in 1972. Clemente was among just nine players back then who had achieved that goal in nearly 100 years of baseball.

Ironically, Roberto Clemente never played another game after his 3,000th hit. His life came to an untimely end during a plane crash a few months later. He was 38 years old. After his death, the world of baseball went to bat for Clemente. The Pirates retired his number and gave his

Clemente became the ninth player to bat 3,000 hits.

In the end, Roberto got the recognition he deserved.

jersey to his wife and his mother. Sportswriters also took the unprecedented step of foregoing the usual five-year wait after a player's last game to consider a player for the Professional Baseball Hall of Fame. Instead, he became in 1973 the first Hispanic player inducted. In the end, Roberto Clemente got the recognition he deserved.

Chapter 2
Destined to Play Ball

The challenges of major league baseball paled in comparison to the life Roberto Walker Clemente knew as a child. Roberto was born about 3:00 P.M. on August 18, 1934, to sugarcane workers in Carolina, Puerto Rico. He was the last of the eight children Luisa and Melchor Clemente raised in a large wooden frame house. The house was located in San Anton, a rural barrio of sugarcane workers surrounded by acres and acres of densely planted sugarcane fields. Luisa and Melchor were hardworking people with strong values. They raised their children with warmth and laughter, despite hardships.

Roberto was the last of the Clementes' eight children.

Roberto with his mother in Puerto Rico

Melchor, age 54 when Roberto was born, worked from sunup until early evening as foreman of sugarcane harvesters. He made 45 cents a day to do dangerous and backbreaking work. As if his day job were not exhausting enough, the tireless Melchor also worked extra hours running a small food business and making deliveries in his truck to provide for his family. His strong work ethic was not lost on Roberto.

When Roberto was a child, Melchor gave him the opportunity to learn the value of hard work. When nine-year-old Roberto asked his father to buy him a used bicycle, Melchor replied, "Earn it." Roberto took his father's words to heart and found a job. He would rise at 5:00 A.M. every day to lug a heavy can of milk half a mile from a neighbor's house to the general store and then take an empty can back. He earned a couple of pennies a day for his labor. In three years he had saved $27 to buy the bike. As a man, recalling the toil of sugarcane workers such as his father often kept Roberto from feeling worn out as a professional baseball player.

"Just think of all those people waking up so early in the morning, cutting cane in the hot sun," Roberto said. "How can I feel tired if all I have to do is play baseball?"

Roberto's mother was a Baptist who regularly brought her children with her to church services. She worked as a laundress and did a variety of jobs to assist in sugarcane production at the Victoria Sugar Mill. Luisa was a dignified woman who remained warm and cheerful despite withstanding tragedy. Her first husband died. Later, their daughter, Rosa Maria, died while giving birth. Another daughter, Ana Iris, died at the age of five after her dress

Recalling the toil of sugarcane workers such as his father often kept Roberto from feeling worn out as a professional baseball player.

accidentally caught on fire. Three of Luisa's children—Luis, Oquendo, and Rosa Maria—were from her first marriage. The other five—Matino, Andres, Osvaldo, Ana Iris, and Roberto—were from her marriage with Melchor. The Clementes were a big family with few resources, but they were happy.

"I was so happy, because my brothers and my father and my mother, we used to get together at night, and we used to sit down and make jokes, and we used to eat whatever we had to eat. And this was something wonderful to me," Roberto said. "I grew up with people who really had to struggle to eat. During the war, when food was hard to get, my parents fed their children first, and they took what was left. They always thought of us. I owe so much to my parents. They did so much for me. I never heard my father or mother raise their voices in our home. I never heard hate in my house."

Roberto's love of baseball distinguished him from his siblings at an early age. He began carrying around a ball and squeezing it when he was five years old to strengthen his hands. He also would throw rubber balls against the wall in his room to practice catching. Roberto's family lacked the money to buy him real baseballs, so Roberto would make his own balls. Sometimes he would wrap string around old golf balls and cover the string with tape. Other times he would crunch old magazines and newspapers, or even socks, into the shape of a ball. Roberto's obsession with baseball so irritated Luisa, especially when he dirtied his best white clothes playing the game on Sundays, that she once tried to burn his bat. Roberto found out and rescued the bat from the flames. Eventually his mother came to realize what Roberto knew in his heart: Roberto was born to play baseball.

"When I was a little kid, the only thing I used to do was play ball all the time," Roberto said. "I started playing baseball in the neighborhood before I was old enough to go to school. We would play all day, and I wouldn't care if we missed lunch. We played until it got so dark that we couldn't see. The more I think about it, I am convinced that God wanted me to play baseball."

Since Roberto's family lacked the money to buy him real baseballs, Roberto made his own balls.

Chapter 3
Becoming a Pro

Clemente was first discovered by Roberto Marín, a scout for a Puerto Rican softball team.

Roberto encountered both fortune and pain on his path to becoming a professional baseball player. A scout for a Puerto Rican softball team first discovered Roberto when he was 14 years old. Roberto and some friends were playing ball on a sandlot, using a stick for a bat and old tin cans for balls. Meanwhile, Roberto Marín was driving the barrios in search of recruits for a team sponsored by the Sello Rojo Rice Company. Roberto's consistent and powerful batting so impressed Marín that he signed Roberto up to play. Finally, Roberto would wear his first uniform, a red-and-white Sello Rojo T-shirt.

Roberto's athletic abilities caused a sensation on the Sello Rojo team, as well as at Julio Vizcarrondo High School in Carolina. Roberto was a perennial all-star shortstop on his school's baseball team, and he was the track team's most valuable member. He could throw a javelin 195 feet and jump six feet high. Coaches considered him a candidate for representing Puerto Rico in track and field in the 1952 Olympic Games in Helsinki, Finland. Instead, baseball kept its hold on Roberto.

Roberto was moving up fast in the baseball world. When he was 16 years old, he moved to a league equal to professional minor leagues in the United States. He played for Juncos, a well-known team in the Double-A League often scouted by minor league teams in the United States and Puerto Rico. When he was 18

Clemente quickly moved from a softball team in Puerto Rico to professional baseball in the United States.

Because of
major
league
rules,
Roberto
had to wait
to enter
the minor
leagues
until he
had
finished
high
school.

years old, on October 9, 1952, he signed a contract to play professional baseball for the Santurce Cangrejeros, or Crabbers, a minor league team in Puerto Rico's winter league.

The owner of the team, Pedrín Zorilla, was a scout for the Brooklyn Dodgers. He invited Roberto to a tryout with Al Campanis, chief Latin American scout for the Dodgers. After seeing 71 players run a 60-yard dash and throw from center field to home plate, Campanis sent everyone home but Roberto. Roberto's impressive hitting sealed Campanis's impression of the young man. Campanis thought Roberto was the greatest natural athlete he had ever seen. He wanted to offer him a minor league contract at that time, but major league rules prevented a prospect from signing a contract until finishing high school. Roberto had one year of school left.

The wait served Roberto well. A year with Santurce helped him polish his skills. Meanwhile, word about his talent got out and several major league scouts pursued him. The interest boiled down to a bidding war between rivals the New York Giants and the Brooklyn Dodgers. Roberto accepted an offer February 19, 1954, from the Dodgers for $5,000 a year with a $10,000 bonus. He

started out playing for the Montreal Royals, the Dodgers' best minor league team. He was an unsuspecting 19-year-old headed for a rude awakening in Canada.

Part of Roberto's trouble was leaving his warm and friendly island for a cold, French-speaking province. Besides his cultural and geographic isolation, the Dodgers did not really want Roberto. They already had a skilled outfield. Instead, they had offered Roberto a contract to keep him from their rival team. They rode him on the bench in the minor leagues to try to break

The Pirates used their first draft pick to purchase Clemente from the Dodgers in 1954.

his spirit and coax him to return home. Roberto did not know that he was being manipulated by the major leagues, and he grew increasingly agitated.

Fortunately, a Pittsburgh Pirates scout, Howie Haak, quelled Roberto's restlessness just in the nick of time. Major league rules allowed the team that finished last each season to acquire a minor league player with a bonus of larger than $4,000. The Pirates were headed for last place, so Haak was keeping an eye on Roberto. He went to visit Roberto in his hotel room after a minor league game during which Roberto rode the bench. Roberto had had enough and was packing his bags for home. Haak, in his broken Spanish, convinced Roberto to hold out until the end of the season when the Pirates could pick him up and, most importantly, play him. Roberto heeded Haak's advice, and Haak remained true to his word. The Pirates used their first draft pick on November 22, 1954, to purchase Roberto Clemente from the Dodgers. Roberto finally landed with a team that would allow him to show the world of professional baseball all he could do.

The Dodgers did not allow Clemente to play, and tried to convince him to return home.

Chapter 4
Love Him or Hate Him

Although Clemente had found a team that became his home, he struggled during his first several seasons with fitting into the world of professional baseball. The team's and his own failure particularly frustrated Clemente during his rookie years in the major leagues. He frequently lost his temper and got kicked out of several games.

On one occasion in 1955, the Pirates' 0-and-8 record so enraged Clemente that he broke 22 of the team's batting helmets with his bat. Manager Fred Haney threatened to fine Roberto $10 a hat if he continued to destroy team property. On another occasion, in 1963, Clemente punched an umpire because he did not agree with the umpire's

The team's failure frustrated Clemente and he frequently lost his temper.

calling him out on a third strike. Roberto thought the ball was outside the plate. He did not get off as easily that time. The National Baseball League president fined him $250 and suspended him for five days.

Also irritating was the racism Roberto encountered on and off the field. During one encounter in New York, a salesman told Clemente he could not afford the furniture he was considering. When Clemente pulled $5,000 out of his wallet and told the salesman who he was, the salesman apologized by saying he thought Clemente was "just another Puerto Rican." Clemente bought neither the explanation nor the furniture.

On the field, Clemente endured racism from teammates and sportswriters alike. Jackie Robinson became the first African-American player in the major leagues in 1947. After he opened the door for minorities, Anglos were uncomfortable with the influx of blacks and Hispanics into major league baseball. No one made racist remarks directly to Clemente, but teammates called black opponents niggers within his earshot.

Sportswriters also showed reluctance to accept Roberto's race. They made fun of his English. They referred to him as Bobby

Sports-writers showed reluctance to accept Roberto's race.

or Bob in print. They called him the Negro bonus player from New York or the Puerto Rican hot dog. Their remarks enraged Clemente, especially because he thought their prejudice hindered them from recognizing his baseball prowess. He was particularly disappointed with their ranking him the eighth best player in the league when the Pirates won the World Series in 1960. He was so hurt he never wore his World Series ring.

Fortunately, Clemente enjoyed a strong connection with the fans. He would spend hours and hours signing autographs because he had nothing else to do during his lonely rookie years. He once took an unemployed factory worker out to dinner after a game, and another time he gave a ride home to a person in a wheelchair. Sometimes he even preferred the company of fans to his teammates. After the Pirates won the seventh game of the World Series in 1960, Clemente changed out of his uniform and celebrated with people in the street rather than with teammates spraying champagne in the locker room.

He laughed with the fans and he cried with them. Tears came to his eyes when presented with the signatures of 300,000

Sometimes Roberto preferred the company of his fans to his teammates.

Roberto signing autographs for two young fans

Puerto Rican fans during Roberto Clemente Night in Pittsburgh in 1970.

In return for their support, Clemente showed great respect to his fans. He dedicated his 3,000th hit "to the fans of Pittsburgh, the people of Puerto Rico and to the man who made me play baseball, Roberto Marín." On another occasion, he tipped his hat, a sign of respect, to the fans when they booed him for making a costly error in right field. Clemente gave everything he had to baseball out of respect for the fans. He thought the fans paid good money to watch a game and deserved to see a good show. He even played in the Puerto Rican winter leagues, when other players rested, because he thought Puerto Rican fans were entitled to watch good players. Once he talked of retiring because an injury hindered him from giving fans the performance they deserved. Without the fans, Roberto felt he was nothing.

"I feel proud when a kid asks me for my autograph," Clemente said. " I send out 20,000 autographed pictures a year to kids. I do it because baseball has given me a good life. Some players complain. I tell them that we do not have to stand in the street with a heavy drill going rat-tat-tat. I believe we owe something to the people who watch us. They work hard for their money. If it wasn't for these fans, I don't know what would have happened to me."

Roberto thought the fans paid good money to watch a game and deserved to see a good show.

Chapter 5
Dying a Hero

After putting Roberto off for several weeks, Vera agreed to date him.

Besides admiration for his athletic abilities, Roberto Clemente was well loved as a human being. He was a loyal son, husband, and father who supported 13 family members on his major league salary. He also championed minority issues and humanitarian causes that eventually cost him his life.

Ironically, the woman who became Roberto's wife had no idea when she met Roberto that he was as special or as famous as he was. Roberto, on the other hand, was sure from the moment he saw Vera Cristina Zabala that he wanted to marry her. He spotted her one day in 1963 in a store back home in Carolina and asked an acquaintance about her. He learned she worked at a bank and decided to call her there, but she would not take his call. Vera came from a respectable family that forbid her from dating, especially someone she did not know, without a chaperone. After putting Roberto off for several weeks, Vera eventually agreed to date him as long as a chaperone accompanied them.

Roberto and Vera were married in 1964.

As the two got acquainted, Roberto learned Vera knew nothing about baseball, and Vera learned by the commotion he created when he visited the bank one day that Roberto was a star. The pair became engaged within nine months of their meeting, and within twelve months they were wed. Nearly 1,500 people attended the church ceremony in Carolina in November 1964. The newlyweds moved into an elegant new house in a wealthy section of Río Piedras. The home sat on top of a hill with dramatic views of distant mountains, the Atlantic Ocean, and San Juan Bay. A trio of boys—Roberto, Jr., Luis, and Enrique—soon followed.

The 1960s were a happy time in Roberto Clemente's professional and family life, but he didn't just sit back and go soft in his contentment. He also gave himself to social causes. Racial issues disturbed him during his entire major league career, and he used whatever platform he could to speak up for minority players. Even when he was on top of his game during the 1966 season, he tried to elevate the status of less recognized but deserving players.

"The Latin American player doesn't get the recognition he deserves," Clemente

Roberto with his wife and three children

said in 1966. "Neither does the Negro player, unless he does something really spectacular, like Willie Mays. We have self-satisfaction, yes, but after the season is over, nobody cares about us. Juan Marichal is one of the greatest players in the game, but does he get invited to banquets? Somebody says we live too far away. That's a lousy excuse. I am an American citizen, but some people act like they think I live in the jungle someplace. To those people, we are outsiders, foreigners."

Besides racism issues, Clemente took up humanitarian causes. Whenever he

Roberto's plane developed engine trouble shortly after takeoff and fell into the sea.

traveled, he showed more interest in getting to know the locals than in tourist attractions. He took particular interest in the poverty of Nicaragua when traveling there in the mid-1960s. The interest turned into a duty in 1972 after a severe earthquake destroyed much of the capital of Managua. Thousands of people were killed or injured. Clemente wanted to help them, so he volunteered to serve as chairperson of the Puerto Rican chapter of the Nicaragua relief effort. He worked tirelessly collecting money, food, clothing, and supplies for the victims. He even went door-to-door asking for donations, and he was determined to deliver the relief himself.

Unfortunately, the rickety old DC-7 cargo plane the relief organization filled with supplies never made it to Nicaragua. The plane developed engine trouble shortly after takeoff and fell into the sea on December 31, 1972. Roberto Clemente's body was never found. The news and mourning over Clemente's death spread so fast that by New Year's Day 1973 thousands of Puerto Ricans silently lined the beach near where the plane crashed. A few days later, fans in the United States and Puerto Rico mourned his death in a joint mass held simultaneously in a downtown Pittsburgh church and the Carolina San Fernando Church, where Roberto had been baptized and married.

Even though fans never saw Roberto bat again, his legacy and generosity have lived on. His death spurred an outpouring of donations that helped make Ciudad Deportiva a reality. Ciudad Deportiva, also known as Roberto Clemente Sports City, is a sports facility Clemente had envisioned that provides recreational opportunities for poor children in Carolina. More than 100,000 children have used the facility, including Ruben Sierra of the Texas Rangers and Dickie Thon of the Philadelphia Phillies, who pays tribute to Clemente by wearing number 21. Indeed, young athletes' use of the facility immortalizes Roberto's vivacious spirit.

Even though fans never saw Roberto bat again, his legacy and generosity have lived on.

Chronology

1934   Roberto Walker Clemente is born August 18 in Carolina, Puerto Rico, to Melchor and Luisa Clemente

1948   Roberto Marín discovers Clemente playing stickball in a sandlot and recruits him to play for the Sello Rojo team

1952   Clemente signs first professional baseball contract with Santurce Cangrejeros (Crabbers) in Puerto Rico

1954   Joins Brooklyn Dodgers' minor league team in Montreal, Canada; leaves the Dodgers for a contract with the Pittsburgh Pirates

1960   Pirates win the World Series after a 33-year lapse; Clemente is ranked a disappointing eighth best player in the National Baseball League

1961   Bats his 1,000th hit; wins his first batting title and his first Gold Glove; plays in his first All-Star Game

1963   Suspended for five days for striking an umpire

1964   Marries Vera Cristina Zabala in Puerto Rico on November 14

1966   Voted Most Valuable Player of the National Baseball League; makes 2,000th hit

1971   Voted Most Valuable Player of the World Series

1972   Bats 3,000th hit on September 30; dies in plane crash off the coast of Puerto Rico on December 31

1973   Becomes the first Puerto Rican baseball player voted into the Professional Baseball Hall of Fame

Index

9/05   1

8/12   1   7/06
5-16   1   ——
8/17   1   ——

1/20   2   9/18
4/21   2   9/14
1/23   2   9/18